Baseball 1st Birthday Party Guest Book

DAISY JOY DESIGNS

Birthday Party Guest List

Birthday Party Guest List

Guest Name and Relationship to Parents

_____

_____

Top Tip For Parents

_____

_____

_____

Special Message to One Year Old

_____

_____

_____

Guest Name and Relationship to Parents

_____

_____

Top Tip For Parents

_____

_____

_____

_____

Special Message to One Year Old

_____

_____

_____

_____

Guest Name and Relationship to Parents

_____

_____

Top Tip For Parents

_____

_____

_____

_____

Special Message to One Year Old

_____

_____

_____

_____

Guest Name and Relationship to Parents

_____

_____

Top Tip For Parents

_____

_____

_____

_____

Special Message to One Year Old

_____

_____

_____

_____

Guest Name and Relationship to Parents

_____

_____

Top Tip For Parents

_____

_____

_____

_____

Special Message to One Year Old

_____

_____

_____

_____

Guest Name and Relationship to Parents

_____

_____

Top Tip For Parents

_____

_____

_____

_____

Special Message to One Year Old

_____

_____

_____

Guest Name and Relationship to Parents

_____

_____

Top Tip For Parents

_____

_____

_____

_____

Special Message to One Year Old

_____

_____

_____

_____

Guest Name and Relationship to Parents

_____

_____

Top Tip For Parents

_____

_____

_____

_____

Special Message to One Year Old

_____

_____

_____

Guest Name and Relationship to Parents

_____

_____

Top Tip For Parents

_____

_____

_____

_____

Special Message to One Year Old

_____

_____

_____

_____

Guest Name and Relationship to Parents

_____

_____

Top Tip For Parents

_____

_____

_____

_____

Special Message to One Year Old

_____

_____

_____

_____

Guest Name and Relationship to Parents

_____

_____

Top Tip For Parents

_____

_____

_____

_____

Special Message to One Year Old

_____

_____

_____

_____

Guest Name and Relationship to Parents

_____

_____

Top Tip For Parents

_____

_____

_____

_____

Special Message to One Year Old

_____

_____

_____

Guest Name and Relationship to Parents

_____

_____

Top Tip For Parents

_____

_____

_____

_____

Special Message to One Year Old

_____

_____

_____

_____

Guest Name and Relationship to Parents

_____

_____

Top Tip For Parents

_____

_____

_____

_____

Special Message to One Year Old

_____

_____

_____

Guest Name and Relationship to Parents

_____

_____

Top Tip For Parents

_____

_____

_____

_____

Special Message to One Year Old

_____

_____

_____

Guest Name and Relationship to Parents

_____

_____

Top Tip For Parents

_____

_____

_____

_____

Special Message to One Year Old

_____

_____

_____

Guest Name and Relationship to Parents

_____

_____

Top Tip For Parents

_____

_____

_____

_____

Special Message to One Year Old

_____

_____

_____

_____

Guest Name and Relationship to Parents

_____

_____

Top Tip For Parents

_____

_____

_____

_____

Special Message to One Year Old

_____

_____

_____

Guest Name and Relationship to Parents

Top Tip For Parents

Special Message to One Year Old

Guest Name and Relationship to Parents

_____

_____

Top Tip For Parents

_____

_____

_____

_____

Special Message to One Year Old

_____

_____

_____

_____

Guest Name and Relationship to Parents

_____

_____

Top Tip For Parents

_____

_____

_____

_____

Special Message to One Year Old

_____

_____

_____

_____

Guest Name and Relationship to Parents

_____

_____

Top Tip For Parents

_____

_____

_____

_____

Special Message to One Year Old

_____

_____

_____

_____

Guest Name and Relationship to Parents

Top Tip For Parents

Special Message to One Year Old

Guest Name and Relationship to Parents

_____

_____

Top Tip For Parents

_____

_____

_____

_____

Special Message to One Year Old

_____

_____

_____

Guest Name and Relationship to Parents

_____

_____

Top Tip For Parents

_____

_____

_____

_____

Special Message to One Year Old

_____

_____

_____

_____

Guest Name and Relationship to Parents

_____

_____

Top Tip For Parents

_____

_____

_____

_____

Special Message to One Year Old

_____

_____

_____

_____

Guest Name and Relationship to Parents

Top Tip For Parents

Special Message to One Year Old

Guest Name and Relationship to Parents

_____

_____

Top Tip For Parents

_____

_____

_____

_____

Special Message to One Year Old

_____

_____

_____

Guest Name and Relationship to Parents

_____

_____

Top Tip For Parents

_____

_____

_____

_____

Special Message to One Year Old

_____

_____

_____

_____

Guest Name and Relationship to Parents

_____

_____

Top Tip For Parents

_____

_____

_____

_____

Special Message to One Year Old

_____

_____

_____

Guest Name and Relationship to Parents

_____

_____

Top Tip For Parents

_____

_____

_____

_____

Special Message to One Year Old

_____

_____

_____

_____

Guest Name and Relationship to Parents

_____

_____

Top Tip For Parents

_____

_____

_____

_____

Special Message to One Year Old

_____

_____

_____

_____

Guest Name and Relationship to Parents

_____

_____

Top Tip For Parents

_____

_____

_____

_____

Special Message to One Year Old

_____

_____

_____

_____

Guest Name and Relationship to Parents

_____

_____

Top Tip For Parents

_____

_____

_____

_____

Special Message to One Year Old

_____

_____

_____

_____

Guest Name and Relationship to Parents

_____

_____

Top Tip For Parents

_____

_____

_____

_____

Special Message to One Year Old

_____

_____

_____

_____

Guest Name and Relationship to Parents

_____

_____

Top Tip For Parents

_____

_____

_____

_____

Special Message to One Year Old

_____

_____

_____

_____

Guest Name and Relationship to Parents

Top Tip For Parents

Special Message to One Year Old

Guest Name and Relationship to Parents

_____

_____

Top Tip For Parents

_____

_____

_____

_____

Special Message to One Year Old

_____

_____

_____

Guest Name and Relationship to Parents

_____

_____

Top Tip For Parents

_____

_____

_____

_____

Special Message to One Year Old

_____

_____

_____

_____

Guest Name and Relationship to Parents

_____

_____

Top Tip For Parents

_____

_____

_____

_____

Special Message to One Year Old

_____

_____

_____

_____

Guest Name and Relationship to Parents

_____

_____

Top Tip For Parents

_____

_____

_____

_____

Special Message to One Year Old

_____

_____

_____

_____

Guest Name and Relationship to Parents

_____

_____

Top Tip For Parents

_____

_____

_____

_____

Special Message to One Year Old

_____

_____

_____

_____

Guest Name and Relationship to Parents

_____

_____

Top Tip For Parents

_____

_____

_____

_____

Special Message to One Year Old

_____

_____

_____

_____

Guest Name and Relationship to Parents

_____

_____

Top Tip For Parents

_____

_____

_____

_____

Special Message to One Year Old

_____

_____

_____

_____

Guest Name and Relationship to Parents

_____

_____

Top Tip For Parents

_____

_____

_____

_____

Special Message to One Year Old

_____

_____

_____

_____

Guest Name and Relationship to Parents

_____

_____

Top Tip For Parents

_____

_____

_____

_____

Special Message to One Year Old

_____

_____

_____

_____

Guest Name and Relationship to Parents

_____

_____

Top Tip For Parents

_____

_____

_____

_____

Special Message to One Year Old

_____

_____

_____

_____

Guest Name and Relationship to Parents

_____

_____

Top Tip For Parents

_____

_____

_____

_____

Special Message to One Year Old

_____

_____

_____

_____

Guest Name and Relationship to Parents

_____

_____

Top Tip For Parents

_____

_____

_____

_____

Special Message to One Year Old

_____

_____

_____

_____

Guest Name and Relationship to Parents

_____

_____

Top Tip For Parents

_____

_____

_____

_____

Special Message to One Year Old

_____

_____

_____

_____

Guest Name and Relationship to Parents

_____

_____

Top Tip For Parents

_____

_____

_____

_____

Special Message to One Year Old

_____

_____

_____

Guest Name and Relationship to Parents

_____

_____

Top Tip For Parents

_____

_____

_____

_____

Special Message to One Year Old

_____

_____

_____

_____

Guest Name and Relationship to Parents

_____

_____

Top Tip For Parents

_____

_____

_____

_____

Special Message to One Year Old

_____

_____

_____

_____

Guest Name and Relationship to Parents

_____

_____

Top Tip For Parents

_____

_____

_____

_____

Special Message to One Year Old

_____

_____

_____

_____

Guest Name and Relationship to Parents

_____

_____

Top Tip For Parents

_____

_____

_____

_____

Special Message to One Year Old

_____

_____

_____

_____

Guest Name and Relationship to Parents

_____

_____

Top Tip For Parents

_____

_____

_____

_____

Special Message to One Year Old

_____

_____

_____

Guest Name and Relationship to Parents

_____

_____

Top Tip For Parents

_____

_____

_____

_____

Special Message to One Year Old

_____

_____

_____

_____

Guest Name and Relationship to Parents

_____

_____

Top Tip For Parents

_____

_____

_____

_____

Special Message to One Year Old

_____

_____

_____

Guest Name and Relationship to Parents

Top Tip For Parents

Special Message to One Year Old

Guest Name and Relationship to Parents

_____

_____

Top Tip For Parents

_____

_____

_____

_____

Special Message to One Year Old

_____

_____

_____

Guest Name and Relationship to Parents

_____

_____

Top Tip For Parents

_____

_____

_____

_____

Special Message to One Year Old

_____

_____

_____

_____

Guest Name and Relationship to Parents

_____

_____

Top Tip For Parents

_____

_____

_____

_____

Special Message to One Year Old

_____

_____

_____

_____

Guest Name and Relationship to Parents

_____

_____

Top Tip For Parents

_____

_____

_____

_____

Special Message to One Year Old

_____

_____

_____

_____

Guest Name and Relationship to Parents

_____

_____

Top Tip For Parents

_____

_____

_____

_____

Special Message to One Year Old

_____

_____

_____

_____

Guest Name and Relationship to Parents

_____

_____

Top Tip For Parents

_____

_____

_____

_____

Special Message to One Year Old

_____

_____

_____

_____

Guest Name and Relationship to Parents

_____

_____

Top Tip For Parents

_____

_____

_____

_____

Special Message to One Year Old

_____

_____

_____

_____

Guest Name and Relationship to Parents

Top Tip For Parents

Special Message to One Year Old

Guest Name and Relationship to Parents

_____

_____

Top Tip For Parents

_____

_____

_____

_____

Special Message to One Year Old

_____

_____

_____

Guest Name and Relationship to Parents

_____

_____

Top Tip For Parents

_____

_____

_____

_____

Special Message to One Year Old

_____

_____

_____

_____

Guest Name and Relationship to Parents

_____

_____

Top Tip For Parents

_____

_____

_____

_____

Special Message to One Year Old

_____

_____

_____

Guest Name and Relationship to Parents

_____

_____

Top Tip For Parents

_____

_____

_____

_____

Special Message to One Year Old

_____

_____

_____

_____

Guest Name and Relationship to Parents

_____

_____

Top Tip For Parents

_____

_____

_____

_____

Special Message to One Year Old

_____

_____

_____

_____

Guest Name and Relationship to Parents

_____

_____

Top Tip For Parents

_____

_____

_____

_____

Special Message to One Year Old

_____

_____

_____

_____

Guest Name and Relationship to Parents

_____

_____

Top Tip For Parents

_____

_____

_____

_____

Special Message to One Year Old

_____

_____

_____

_____

Guest Name and Relationship to Parents

_____

_____

Top Tip For Parents

_____

_____

_____

_____

Special Message to One Year Old

_____

_____

_____

_____

Guest Name and Relationship to Parents

Top Tip For Parents

Special Message to One Year Old

Guest Name and Relationship to Parents

_____

_____

Top Tip For Parents

_____

_____

_____

_____

Special Message to One Year Old

_____

_____

_____

_____

Guest Name and Relationship to Parents

_____

_____

Top Tip For Parents

_____

_____

_____

_____

Special Message to One Year Old

_____

_____

_____

_____

Guest Name and Relationship to Parents

_____

_____

Top Tip For Parents

_____

_____

_____

_____

Special Message to One Year Old

_____

_____

_____

_____

Guest Name and Relationship to Parents

_____

_____

Top Tip For Parents

_____

_____

_____

_____

Special Message to One Year Old

_____

_____

_____

_____

Guest Name and Relationship to Parents

_____

_____

Top Tip For Parents

_____

_____

_____

_____

Special Message to One Year Old

_____

_____

_____

_____

Guest Name and Relationship to Parents

_____

_____

Top Tip For Parents

_____

_____

_____

_____

Special Message to One Year Old

_____

_____

_____

_____

Guest Name and Relationship to Parents

_____

_____

Top Tip For Parents

_____

_____

_____

_____

Special Message to One Year Old

_____

_____

_____

_____

Guest Name and Relationship to Parents

Top Tip For Parents

Special Message to One Year Old

Guest Name and Relationship to Parents

_____

_____

Top Tip For Parents

_____

_____

_____

_____

Special Message to One Year Old

_____

_____

_____

_____

Guest Name and Relationship to Parents

Top Tip For Parents

Special Message to One Year Old

Guest Name and Relationship to Parents

_____

_____

Top Tip For Parents

_____

_____

_____

_____

Special Message to One Year Old

_____

_____

_____

_____

Guest Name and Relationship to Parents

_____

_____

Top Tip For Parents

_____

_____

_____

_____

Special Message to One Year Old

_____

_____

_____

_____

Guest Name and Relationship to Parents

_____

_____

Top Tip For Parents

_____

_____

_____

_____

Special Message to One Year Old

_____

_____

_____

_____

Guest Name and Relationship to Parents

_____

_____

Top Tip For Parents

_____

_____

_____

_____

Special Message to One Year Old

_____

_____

_____

_____

Guest Name and Relationship to Parents

_____

_____

Top Tip For Parents

_____

_____

_____

_____

Special Message to One Year Old

_____

_____

_____

_____

Guest Name and Relationship to Parents

_____

_____

Top Tip For Parents

_____

_____

_____

_____

Special Message to One Year Old

_____

_____

_____

_____

Guest Name and Relationship to Parents

Top Tip For Parents

Special Message to One Year Old

Guest Name and Relationship to Parents

_____

_____

Top Tip For Parents

_____

_____

_____

_____

Special Message to One Year Old

_____

_____

_____

_____

Guest Name and Relationship to Parents

_____

_____

Top Tip For Parents

_____

_____

_____

_____

Special Message to One Year Old

_____

_____

_____

_____

Guest Name and Relationship to Parents

_____

_____

Top Tip For Parents

_____

_____

_____

_____

Special Message to One Year Old

_____

_____

_____

Guest Name and Relationship to Parents

Top Tip For Parents

Special Message to One Year Old

Guest Name and Relationship to Parents

_____

_____

Top Tip For Parents

_____

_____

_____

_____

Special Message to One Year Old

_____

_____

_____

Guest Name and Relationship to Parents

_____

_____

Top Tip For Parents

_____

_____

_____

_____

Special Message to One Year Old

_____

_____

_____

_____

Guest Name and Relationship to Parents

_____

_____

Top Tip For Parents

_____

_____

_____

_____

Special Message to One Year Old

_____

_____

_____

_____

Picture Memories

Picture Memories

Picture Memories

Picture Memories

Picture Memories

Bonus Gift Package

DOWNLOADABLE PRINTABLE GIFT TRACKER

HTTP://BIT.LY/BIRTHDAY-GIFT-TRACKER

Made in the USA
Middletown, DE
17 April 2022